I can finger paint

Ray Gibson

Designed and illustrated by Amanda Barlow
Edited by Jenny Tyler

Contents

Spotty spiders

1. Dip your finger in paint. Go around and around to make a body.

2. Draw 8 legs with a fingertip dipped in paint.

3. Do some big white eyes. Put a dark dot in each one.

You can mix your paint with flour to make it thicker and dry quicker.

4. Dab bright spots all over.

3

Cats

1. Go around and around with a painty finger for a body.

2. Add a smaller head.

3. Do the ears and tail with a fingertip.

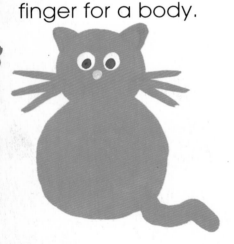

4. Add whiskers. Do eyes and nose with a fingertip.

5. Dab white paint on the cheeks, chest and feet.

5

Rainbow fish

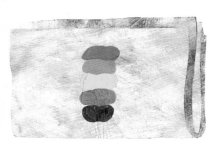

1. Spoon different paints close together on newspaper.

2. Press your hand on the paint and then on the paper.

3. Turn the shape around. Paint a tail with your finger.

4. Add an eye, and bright spots.

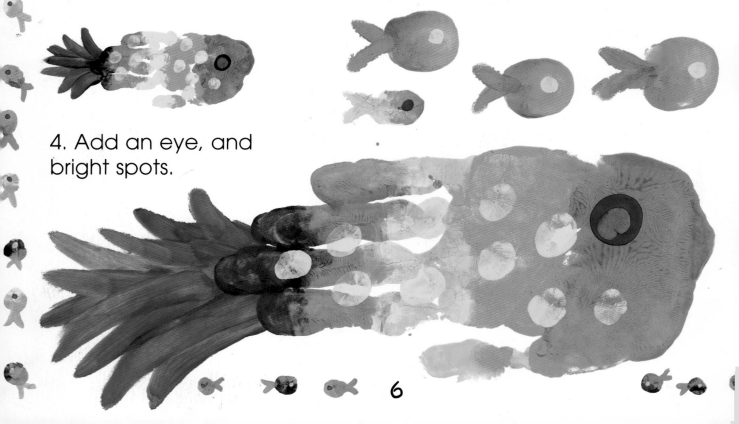

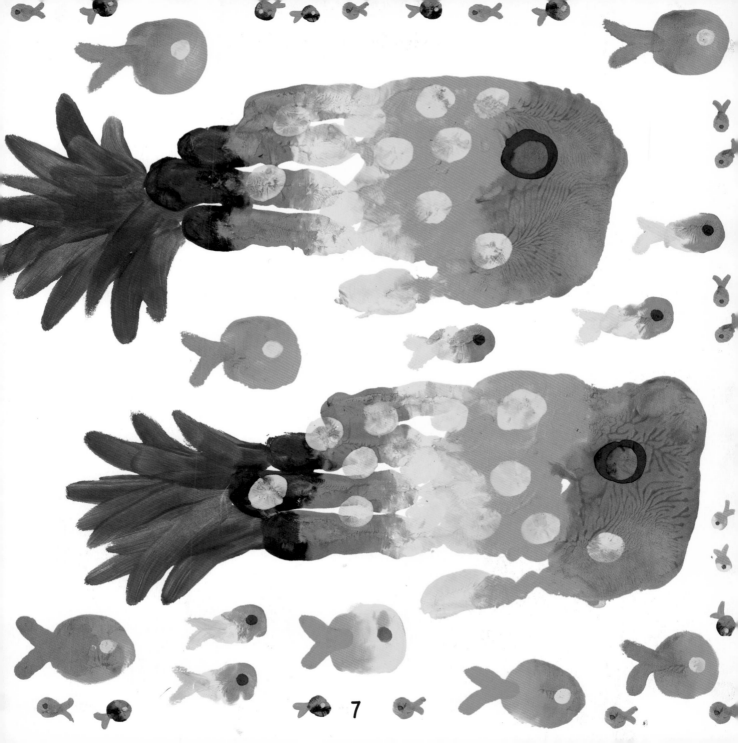

7

A folding pattern

1. Fold some paper.
Open out. Press
your hand in paint.

2. Press your hand
on one side of the
paper.

3. Wash your hands.
Fold the paper. Press
it all over.

8

4. Open out. Add more patterns on one side.

5. Fold and press again. Open it out.

6. Finger paint more patterns with different paints.

9

A rocket

1. Cut a long shape from newspaper for the rocket. Tear cloud shapes.

2. Dip them in water. Let them drip. Press them onto plain paper.

3. Pat blue paint over with your hand.

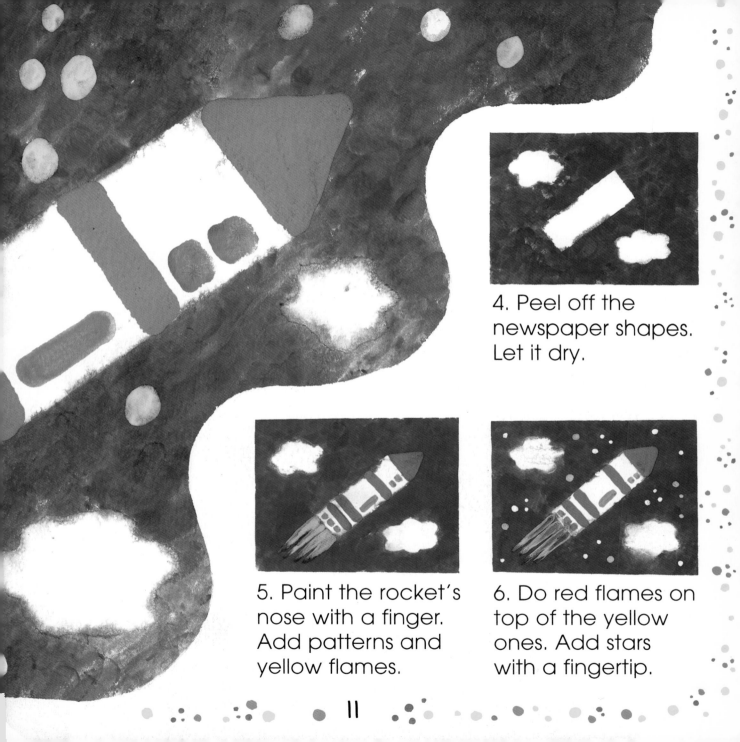

4. Peel off the newspaper shapes. Let it dry.

5. Paint the rocket's nose with a finger. Add patterns and yellow flames.

6. Do red flames on top of the yellow ones. Add stars with a fingertip.

Lots of flowers

1. Dip your finger in purple paint.

2. Make blue dots around the purple one.

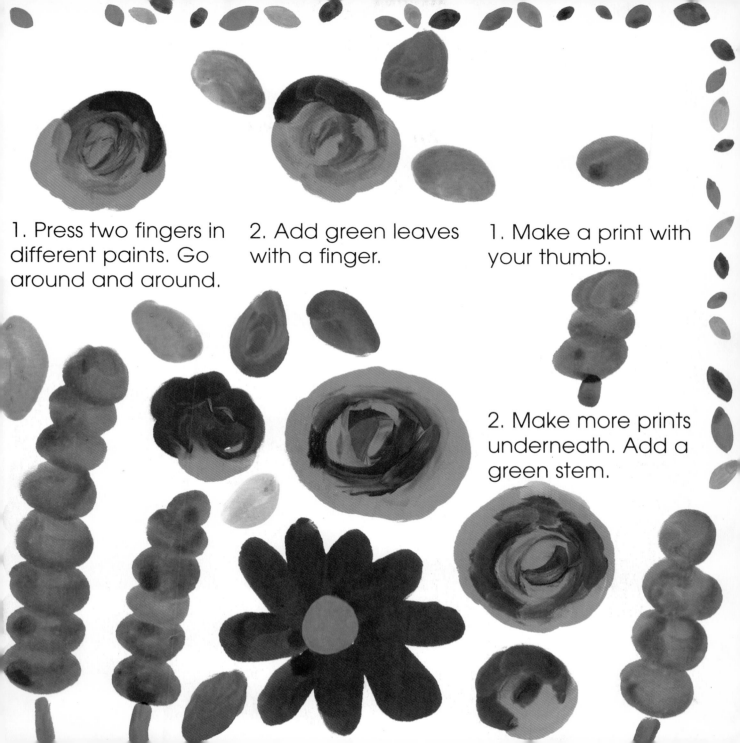

1. Press two fingers in different paints. Go around and around.

2. Add green leaves with a finger.

1. Make a print with your thumb.

2. Make more prints underneath. Add a green stem.

An owl in a tree

1. Wet some paper with your hand. Rub yellow, orange and red paint on, like this.

2. Dip your finger in black paint. Use it to paint a tree trunk.

3. Add some long branches, using more black paint.

4. Do small branches and a hedge along the bottom.

5. Do an owl in the tree. Give him big eyes.

6. Paint a moon with your finger. Dot on some stars.

Field of rabbits

1. Press yellow handprints all over your paper. Add green handprints.

2. Finger paint a fat sausage on top for a rabbit's body.

3. Add the head.

Dab on flowers with a fingertip

4. Finger paint ears and legs.

5. Do a white tail.

Lots of shapes

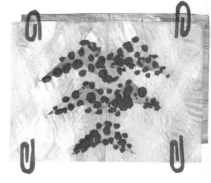

1. Fold a piece of paper in half. Cut some shapes out of the folded side.

2. Open it out. Paper clip it onto another piece of paper.

3. Dot paint over the shapes with your fingertip.

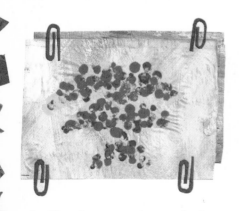

4. Dot more paint on top so the shapes are covered.

5. Lift off the top sheet to see the pattern.

19

Snails in a puddle

1. Wet some paper with your hand. Dip your fingers in paint. Make watery patterns. Let them dry.

2. Use different paper. Make a green circle with your finger.

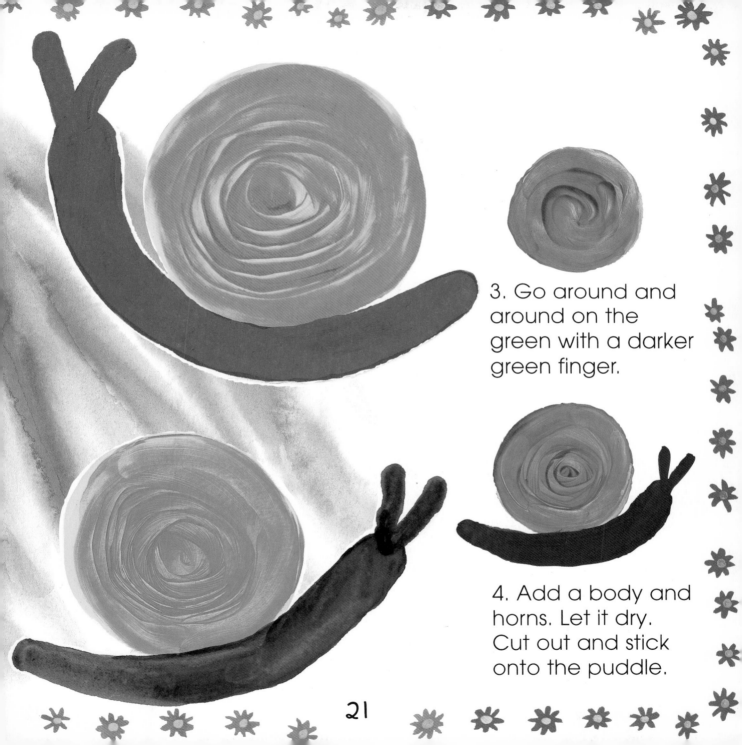

3. Go around and around on the green with a darker green finger.

4. Add a body and horns. Let it dry. Cut out and stick onto the puddle.

21

An iceberg picture

1. Tear an iceberg shape from the edge of newspaper. Wet it.

2. Lay it on paper, like this. Add more shapes.

3. Dip your hands in blue paint. Pat them all over.

4. Add some green, then a little white.

5. Peel off the shapes carefully to see the icebergs.

6. Paint a canoe with a finger. Add some fishermen.

An angel

1. Make a whole handprint in the middle. This is an upside-down dress.

2. Make two whole hand prints a bit lower, for the wings.

3. Turn your paper. Go around and around with your finger for a head.

4. Use your fingertip to do arms and hands.

5. Finger paint some hair and a halo.

6. Dot on some eyes, and a nose. Paint a smiling mouth.

An alligator

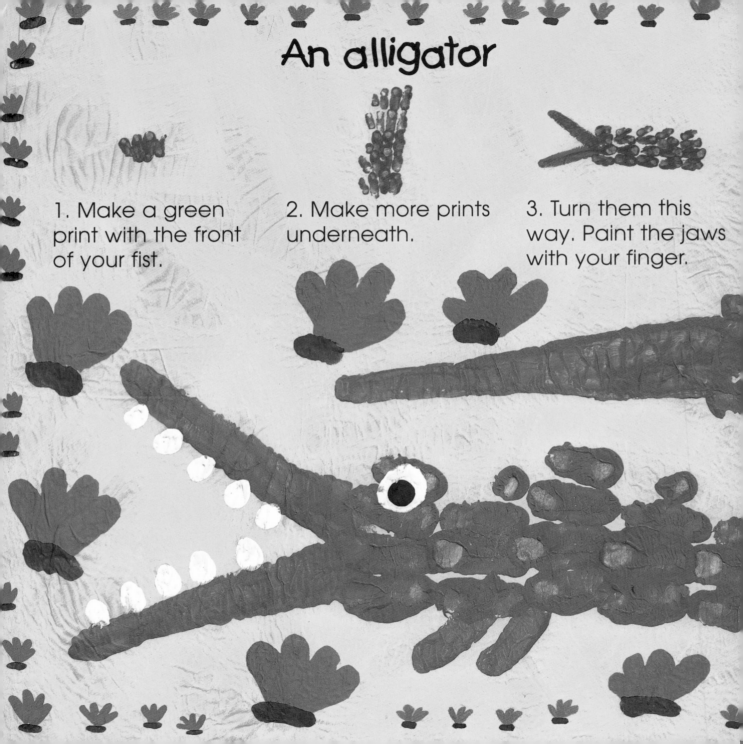

1. Make a green print with the front of your fist.

2. Make more prints underneath.

3. Turn them this way. Paint the jaws with your finger.

Add a long tail
nd four legs.

5. Make dots for
teeth along the
jaws.

6. Dot a white
eye with a black
middle.

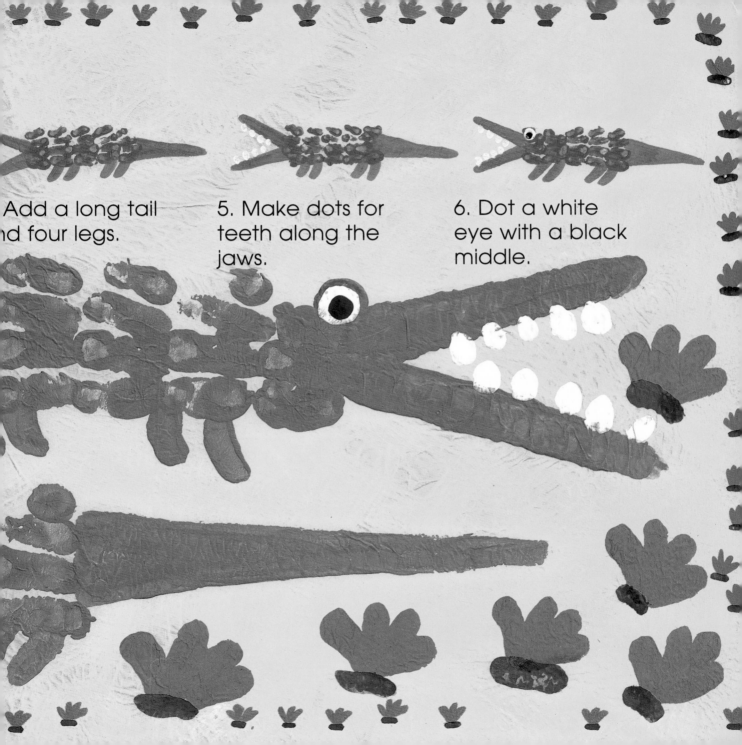

Spiky animals

1. Dip your fingertip in paint. Go around and around for a body.

2. Make one end pointed for a snout.

3. Add an eye and a nose with your fingertip.

4. Finger paint spikes all over his back.

A jungle picture

1. Wet a large piece of paper. Let it drip.

2. Finger paint a green dot. Add leaves around it.

3. Do more of these in dark and light green. Leave to dry.

4. Paint a bird body with a finger. Add wings.

5. Dot a beak, the ends of the wings and tail. Add an eye.

6. Use your finger to dot on jungle flowers.

Funny creatures

1. Go around and around with a finger dipped in paint to make a blob.

2. Do spikes all around with different paint.

3. Add eyes, legs and feet with a fingertip.

First published in 1997 by Usborne Publishing Ltd, 83-85 Saffron Hill, London EC1N 8RT, England.
Copyright © 1997 Usborne Publishing Ltd. The name Usborne and the device ♀ are Trade Marks of Usborne Publishing Ltd. All rights reserved. No part of this publication may be reproduced, stored in a retrieval system, or transmitted in any form or by any means, electronic, mechanical, photocopy, recording or otherwise, without prior permission of the publisher. Printed in Portugal